My Sister June

Written by Deborah Eaton

Illustrated by Elizabeth Allen

My big sister June is lots of fun.

She always plays with me.

June and I like to jump in mud puddles.

One day I jumped in a huge mud puddle.

Dad said, "June! What are you up to now?"

June and I like to be a band.

One day I played my drum on
the school bus.

The bus driver said, "June! What are you
up to now?"

June and I like to do art stuff.

One day I cut up the newspaper.

I tried to glue it, but then the wind blew.

Mr. Moon said, "June! What are you up to now?"

June and I like to play with our
baby brother.

One day I blew up a balloon.

Then I popped it.

Mom said, "June! What are you up to now?"

June and I like to fix up our room.

One day I cut out huge white clouds.

Then I painted the wall blue.

Oops! Big blue drips!

Mom came into the room.

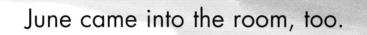

June came into the room, too.

Mom said, "Jessica Beth! What are you up to now?"